OTHER BOOKS BY TOM LYFORD:

~ CHAPBOOKS ~

Pleasant Street: A Chapbook of Baby Boomer Ballads & Poems (2005)

Poetic License (2005)

On Becoming a Man of Substance: The Adventure (2006)

Americana (2006)

Kilroy Was Here: Me Too! (2009)

~ MEMOIR ~

Work Aversion Trauma: A Lifetime of Suffering (2009)

MY
CINEMA
PARADISO

BY TOM LYFORD

Green Bough Publishing
121 Pleasant Street
Dover-Foxcroft, ME 04426

Cover art by author

Printed and bound by
www.createspace.com

Subjects within include: 1. Poetry;
2. Memoir; 3. Biography; 4. Movie references;
5. The film buff's perspective

ISBN 978-0-9827016-0-7

www.tomlyford.com

~DEDICATION~

My Cinema Paradiso
is dedicated to the memory of

ANN MacKINNON KUCERA

~December 18th, 1925 - November 18th, 2009~
my crusty, humorous, inspirational old friend who
once said of my poetry, "Why, this is doggerel…
and doggerel is poetry written by dogs!"
How I miss you, Ann!

~ACKNOWLEDGEMENTS~

Special thanks to my copy editor and good friend
Iris Snowfire
for her expertise, input, and encouragement…

The following poems, under different titles, have
been featured in these publications respectively:

"Easter Parade"	*Bangor Daily News*
"High Plains Drifter"	*Wolf Moon Journal*
"It Happens Every Spring"	*Village Soup*
"The Lost World"	*Bangor Daily News*
"North to Alaska"	*Village Soup*
"The Right Stuff"	*Off the Coast*
"The River of No Return"	*Bangor Metro*
"The Trojan Women"	*Bangor Daily News*

NOTE: Nearly all of the poems in this volume, also
under different titles, have appeared earlier in the
author's five published chapbooks.

TABLE OF CONTENTS

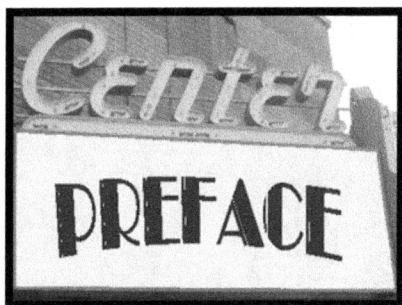

CINEMA PARADISO

It begins with vulnerable *me,* Pinocchio-tall,
hand-led, all eyes and ears and nose-a-tingle,
my virgin sneakers scuffing the stampede-
worn, musty magic-kingdom carpet down

the velvet-roped gallery of lurid posters...
siren posters singing in silence, singing me
dizzily forward beyond my years, singing me
back fridaysaturdaysunday, singing me

sugarplums of dynamited railroad trestles,
riders hellbent-for-leather, bare-knuckled
brawls fought over damsels in the dust
above the ripped-bodice cleavage and

always, always... the naked thigh
titillating... tantalizing me down
the tilted funhouse floor into the
electric-yellow popcorn dark...

my Rip Van Winkle real life
leashed to a parking meter and
left languishing in the black and
white sunshine outside...

ALIAS JESSE JAMES

Sprung from the maternity ward on or about
the same day, blood-brothers cursed with
good ol' boys' curiosities, just a natural-born
Frank and Jesse James gang of two, our first
heists being valve-stem caps off the tires of
idling cars parked out front of Bob Roberts'
Grocery only because they were *there* I guess
and something we could reach... our trikes
growing then into bikes with horses' names,
later developing into Harleys engined by aces
of spades clothes-pinned right into the spokes
flacketty-rackettywhack!

Short and invisible to adults in the fall of '58...
slipping under the radar through the gala open-
house crowd in the back of the Dover Motor
Chevrolet showroom and brazenly peeking up the
canvas skirt shrouding the about-to-be-unveiled
Car of the Future, us becoming the absolute *first
human beings on the planet!* to eyeball the
Oh-my-God, drop-dead super fins of the '59...
Purple Heart veterans of the Merrick Square Pea-
shooter Campaign of the early '60s that escalated
into savage backyard guerilla warfare where
the weapon of choice was the apple-grenade
speared onto the sharp tip of a limbed sapling
and propelled with a quick fierce *whip-snap!*

And always looking to the likes of Bogart
and Cagney for what to say and how to say it,
or how to smoke those stolen ashtray butts...
wondering about S-E-X... and
just *itching* to get older...

3

ALTERED STATES

Cousin to the copier…
I commiserate with
office machines

whose red warning lights
flash *TONER: LOW!*
(I know how this feels).

My warning lights
have often flashed
SEROTONIN: LOW!

The toner-deficient copier
Produces mere spotty outlines
of intended concepts.

Serotonin-deficient, my
verbal output drops to
barely perfunctory monosyllables.

But somebody always goes to
Supply and pops a brand new
cartridge into the slot.

I always go
to the cabinet and
pop my capsule.

The copier prints
state-of-the-art graphics.
I am *gregarious!*

THE ARRIVAL

Up here in the boondocks in the summer
of '52, television was still out there
somewhere... somewhere *else*, but not
here... out there in New York, Boston...
but not here where radios ruled our
backwoods living rooms— consoles

big enough for Sidney Greenstreet
to hide behind. And like rumors of
war, there were whispers: *It is coming...*
It was in the headlines, the editorials,
Television's on the way! It's almost here!
It was on the radio: *Any day now!*

And then one night just at dusk,
we spied the crowd gathered like
penguins in the snow out in front of
Ward's department store... everybody
gawking at a luminous little round
'screen' in the big picture window!

BACK TO THE FUTURE

—In 1956, Miss O'Brien fibrillated my tender ten-
year-old heart with an apocalyptic woodcut print,
the *show* of her show-and-tell: the hapless denizens
of 1910 cowering beneath a fiery eye in the sky…
"Halley's comet returns every seventy-five years,"
she concluded pertly, me eyeing the calendar
dreading that Flash Gordonish future of 1986…

—In 1960 I shuddered over Orwell's *1984*
and switched instead to escapist time machine
sagas, seeking escape hatches back to
the safe and familiar past…

—In 1968, *2001: A Space Odyssey* left me
with this heart-pounding epiphany:
The only *good* computer— a *dead* one!
Get them *before* they get you!

But 1984 turned out to be just another day in
paradise, and Comet Halley a virtual no-show.
By 2001, I was 'shot-gunning' the hell out of
Duke Nukem on my seventh PC, a benign drone
that couldn't be more shuffling and subservient
if I were Flash Gordon's powerful nemesis,
Ming the Merciless… and meanwhile…

My 64th birthday is a pocked space rock
hurtling through deep space, a rogue asteroid
with my name on it… and it's T-minus three
hundred days to impact! Me? I'm just happily
humming 'When I'm Sixty-Four' right along
with the long-defunct Beatles… ho-hum…

THE BEAT GENERATION

Beatnik-wannabe child of the 50's
the black and white days, craving
the uniform: black turtleneck,
black beret, threadworn chinos,
torn sneakers, bongos and shades…

born too early in a *Father Knows Best*,
Leave It to Beaver sitcom; the Western
Auto, A&P store boondocks— America's
Dreamsville— fine-tuning my precocious
senses to the underground frequencies, the

subliminal previews of Coming Attractions: the
siren whispers about the Oz called The Village,
the café-nicotine poetry, the Princes of Darkness,
Kerouac and Ginsberg, their Beat Generation
already setting sail in the Elsewhere-ville sunset

leaving me behind: a stranger on the
shore of my youth: off the road, off the
bus, praying those cool daddy-o mantras,
trying to kickstart my peachfuzz, needing
to be weird-with-a-beard in
the Land of the Beard Nazis

THE BIG CHILL

You are the spark that ignited
the fuse for the Big Bang of my
hitherto relatively uneventful love life…
it flashing all incendiary! All Roman candles
and rockets! Molotov-cocktail love!
Flame-thrower love! Burning magnesium hot
and launching me in a straight trajectory
right over Lover's Leap at $E=mc^2$…

But that was in my callow youth…
Today, like the perpetual
Olympic flame, my love
for you still burns—
patient now and serene…
electric blanket warm…
cup of cocoa hot…
fireplace cozy…

THE BIG HEAT

Still at large… on the lam
after all these long years…
the poet in me *rats me out,*

offers me a plea bargain...
places my hands on my head
and escorts me at gunpoint

out into the siren-searchlights
where I… *Freeze! Up against*
the wall! Assume the stance!

And in the hallowed halls of
The Poetic Justice Department…
beneath the bare lightbulb…

strapped into the polygraph's
hot-seat and other hardware of
your goodcop-badcop world…

I sing like a canary
spill my guts
name names

on thousands of blank pages…
into hundreds of open mic's…
Look, I'm cooperatin', see?

Yeah, yeah, I know—
anything I say 'can and
will be used against me '—

but these is my stories, see?
and I'm stickin' to 'em…
See?

BLACK*BIRD* JUNGLE

My hush puppies propped up between
the mountains of uncorrected essays and
paperbacks, a desk on the brink of avalanche—
two minutes and counting till Pavlov's bell

tolls for me, thee, for period three, and this
free-period reverie: gazing out the window upon
legions of sparrows flocking, and doing what
sparrows *do*: pecking out free-lunch livings like

lilies of the field who toil *not*… and me conned
into this *To Sir With Love* scam, wondering
how a goddamn field lily feels anyway. When
flocks of blackbirds roll in *en masse* like

jack-booted Hells Angels rumbling into
Weir's Beach, spreading the black stain of
Biker Week to roust these pathetic, tweedy, little
checker-breasted and pocket-protectored

peaceniks in a scene right out of *The Wild One*…
and suddenly bells harangue the halls, my door
slams wide open, and I too am rousted by my
all-male period-four easy riders, birds of a

uniform feather in sleeveless Levi jacket-vests
with 'EXILES' stamped boldly in bad-ass biker
font across the backs and reeking reefer madness,
the pockets nested with seeds and stems…

BLUE COLLAR

Want ads… the tiny textprint turnstiles
fronting timespace wormholes through
the wild-blue-collar cosmos yonder

yawning like caverns you want
to explore… but don't want to
go permanently *missing* in…

little classified 'green-door' gateways
where, if you knock the knock and
it turns out Joe sent you, they might

just let you slip on past into
some bizarro, parallel-world,
sitcom *screen* test where…

the same old you could land a
whole new wardrobe-makeover…
hard hat and steel-toed boots…

and join a whole brand new cast of characters
all directed by still yet some other nemesis…
a new Little Napoleon or Captain Ahab

CARS

This body you got?
          that you found yourself seat-belted in
          like some little red Radio Flyer
          that night you came-to in the OB ward...
this body you bombed around the
planet in like some high-octane
babe-magnet Triumph SR3 fueled
          on the endless river of hormones
          running through it, all piss and
          vinegar and adrenaline... this body
that lusted for all those other sweet young
candy-apple-cute showroom models
cruising the strip all chromed up?

This body you're stuck in now?
          with the snowball's chance in hell of getting
          one more inspection sticker? that you kick
          yourself for not servicing more regularly?
this body no silver-tongued used-car
dealer could foist on anything loftier
than the local parts-salvage junkyard?

This body being towed at the end of your parade?
          it's waxing you philosophical, am I right?
          helping you work on letting go, on sitting
          back and just enjoying the scenery of all
that mileage disappearing like some Triple-A
travelogue slide-show-in-reverse in the
rearview mirror... leaving you lost in your
          Lake Wobegon dealership dreams...
          where all the models are good lookin'...
          and all the warranties above average...

CONTACT

Think of the parade of moons
that have wheeled over this roof
over our slumber… *legions* of
moons, while we, joined at the hip—
>*yours so warm*
>*in the blankets*
>*pressed to mine*

while we've reposed at the mercy
of our respective funhouse dream-
scapes having their way with us…
and always our contact points
>communicating electrically
>communicating chemically
>in the Big Midnight of the

Big Sleep— *you're here…*
answering *I'm here…* affirming
we're both of us here
and everything is alright…
>*and, just for now, it doesn't matter*
>*that we don't know how it will all*
>*turn out in the final reel…*

THE CREATURE WALKS AMONG US

The Pleasant Street Phantom (us poor boys'
Abominable Snowman) cannonballed out
of the wild blue blazes, ran ripshod through
the flashlight-tag magic of the lightning-bug
twinkledark— its hair-raising hellhound
howl sending us all into spin-tizzies...

turned us into torch-wielders mobbing after him
down dark sidewalks under the streetlamps all
gasps, shrieks and belly-giggles trying to catch
him, catch a good glimpse, put a name on him...
on *it*... and vanished right before our eyes under
the old apple tree... only a voice remaining...

taunting us ventriloquently, his wild spook-dark
war whoops from the north, south, east and west—
and years later, this indelibly delicious myth... this
neighborhood urban legend, longed-for during the
light... turned out (eventually) (in time) to be
(by confession) only Gaylon Richards...

next-door-neighbor track star
ten years my senior who once,
under a blue-afternoon-sky-sun,
raced me down Pleasant Street Hill
(him on foot and me *on my bike!*) and
smoked me by three bicycle lengths!

DARK STAR

Surrounded by advancing, devil-dancing pygmy cannibals...
Jungle Jim saves the blonde bombshell by recalling The
Information Please Almanac's *prediction of the total eclipse of*
the sun conveniently one minute before it occurs... just in time
to deliver his climactic ultimatum: "You no lay-ee down
weapons? Me take-ee way sun!" And the rest, of course, is
campy, cinematic history—

Thus did I begin to romance the grandeur
of the Celestial Clockworks...

and finally at long, *long* last... as foretold in the
tom-toms of our ancient astronomic calendars and
codices, there came to pass along the 45th parallel
on my seventeenth swing 'round the summer sun, a
total eclipse in *my* timespace continuum that turned
downtown Dexter into a Mayan Mecca swollen
with sun-worshipping eclipse-chasers offering up
sacrifices of dance and joyful noise, exotic pilgrims
from the Seven Seas posturing their Pentaxes and
Pilgrimatics in a United Nations' shutterbug-
encampment... a forest of transient tripods—

but on a mile-away farm, I get to feel first-hand
the Apocalyptic Horseman Approach of *Totality*...
witness the wondrous and clumsy panic of the
cattle lurching hurriedly for the mid-day barn
before the rapidly falling Old Testament Dark
confused as any silver-screen headhunters whose
world the gods have damned to annihilation—
and a chill like the Shadow of Death in this
noon-black midnight generates (even in *me*)
an unexpected God *fearing*— but then the cows
are plodding back to pasture, the salmon sky grows
blue again, and somewhere... a rooster crows.

15

DAYS OF WINE AND ROSES

Born imprisoned in Original Sin
I wanted out…

Born across the street from The Green Door
I wanted in…

Born into Puritanism
I lusted flamboyantly…

Born tangled up in Mom's apron strings
I fantasized Cool Risks…

Born to fantasize myself The Hero
I died The Coward's Thousand Deaths…

Born required to confess
I lied like a politician… and

Born in The Temperance League's headquarters
I drank myself gratefully under the table…

THE DEEP

Following the treasure maps
of dreams and flashbacks, I
dive the murky fathoms down
again and again to hover weightless
above the derelict hulks of my
childhood rusting on the ocean floor
of deep-sixed memories dotting, with
their artifactual debris, a past that
once seemed to have vanished in
the Bermuda Triangle of
Time's Crosscurrents…

Only outlines remain discernable now
beneath the silt of decades: the heirloom
compass I refused to steer by, the anchor
whose chain I severed in mutiny, and
the barnacled cannons I fired
with malice during the historic
Angry Young Man Rebellions…

They're all,
all down there
skulking like
groupers in grottoes…
the bones of the
Davy Jones' locker
I rifle through to
harvest my poems
like pearls and
pieces of
eight

DELIVERANCE

A
lost
parcel
in the Cosmic Limbo
of Life's Dead Letter Office,
I languished a lifetime under
a plain brown wrapper skin
keeping your prying eyes
off my lurid cover right
up until I attempted
suicide with the
letter-opener of
desperation

and
found
that I wasn't
so 'fragile' after all…
found that what doesn't
handle you with care makes
you stronger… found that
my bad news wasn't so bad…
found that come rain,
sleet, snow, or hail
you can still
anticipate
delivery

DR. JECKYLL AND MR. HYDE

It's a constant audition, this balancing act
of Good and Evil, with the Seven Deadly Sins
and Sainthood waiting in the wings,
lurking, like loan sharks… and
virtue is its own reward, but…
something wicked this way comes!

So how does the soul finally decide
with Mother Teresa on the right
shoulder and Charlie Manson on the
left… this left brain right brain thing…
this yin and yang of Cain and Abel
of Jeckyll and Hyde?

DIAMONDS ARE FOREVER

Lucky Superman who, in the
black and white re-runs, can
hand-squeeze a lump of coal
into a beautiful professionally-
cut diamond, short-cutting the
millennium-long process down
to a matter of thirty seconds!

In the mother-of-pearl lining of
our passionate relationship's
ulcerated womb... barnacled
with the Samsonite baggage
of fear, insanity, insecurity,
dysfunction, codependency,
cruelty, rage, and addictions...

Time has finally festered
a pearl of great price

EARTH VS.THE FLYING SAUCERS

We are not alone!
They're *here!*
(*They've always been here!*)
Monitoring us from Atlantean
Bermuda-Triangle fortresses...
*extra*terrestrials and *intra*terrestrials
in UFO's and **U**nidentified
Submerged **O**bjects!

We are not alone. Oh, we jacked
one of theirs at *Roswell*; of course,
they nabbed our Flight 19... watch it
on The History Channel (*and check
out those Plains of Nazca!*) or just ask
Von Daniken, or Betty and Barney Hill,
Or Mulder and Scully (*but not the Men in
Black... they won't talk about The Greys!*)

We are not alone. They cultivate us
like peas (*PODS!*); they abduct us
(*BODY SNATCHERS!*); re-splice our
genes (*X-FILES!*); mix and match us
(*CATTLE MUTILATIONS!*); and graft us
like apples and oranges in
some hideous, insidious
Plan-9 (*FROM OUTER SPACE!*)

(*Sing it, Major Tom!*)

*'And I'm floating in a most peculiar way...
and the stars look very dif...fer...ent today...'*

21

EASTER PARADE

Every sunrise but the Sabbath
the faithful stationed along the route
anticipate my arrival like a prophecy—
the coming of The Promised One

and house by house, by ones and twos,
the pre-leash law pinscher and pointer,
the beagle, boxer, and bassett… and
Judas the Jack Russell 'doubting' terrier

wagging their windshield-wiper tails,
watering telephone poles righteously
sniffing butts and helping lawns
to be fertile and prosper…

join me, casting aside their nets…
casting their lots instead with *me,*
their suburban *Jesus du Jour,* swaddled
in newspaper delivery-sack cloth…

missionaries of the word—
my dozen disciples delivering
the Good (*Bangor Daily*) News…
barking their happy *Hosannahs!*

THE FLIGHT OF THE PHOENIX

When Rehab Dave, the hotshot Jesus of
the fourth floor counseling staff first laid
his 'flight mechanic' eyes on the fractured
fuselage and flamed-out, bullet-ridden engines
of my crash-landed so-called *life* languishing
there among the other soul-less hulks of rusting
warbirds up there in the graveyard ward...

he began poking around in my twisted metal
with the enthusiasm of a fool on a fool's errand,
laying out his 'wrenches and welding tools' with
mechanical obliviousness to my ranting and
righteous Jimmy Stewart indignation over the
obvious and goddamn pointlessness of it all!
but... in the end... well...

the sonuvagun knew something
about raising the dead after all...

THE FULL MONTY

You commence with an ultra-safe
picture-postcard piece from your
little patchwork poetry quilt of
Norman Rockwellian Americana…
just to get your foot in the door…
and yeah— now they know you're
alive up here at least… they're
settling down and settling in with
that good old obligatory applause—

but then off the top of your repertoire
you doff something slightly prurient…
scale it like a Chippendale hardhat
out over the coffeehouse darkness and
the chatter and clink of churning spoons…
and their eyes lock-on because suddenly
you're the Reality Show Network and
they're looking just a tad *what*, embarrassed
for you perhaps? yeah— but interested…

but for you, this is adrenal, this is liberating—
risky though, like oops, your soul's little bald
spot is reflecting in the spotlight like a chrome
hubcap and you're simultaneously burning with
self-consciousness and breathing a sigh of relief
like the comb-over guy who finally gets a real
haircut, but hey— whatever doesn't *kill* you
makes you stronger, right… the truth will
set you free… so up next: a sassy little

indiscretion from your dark, drunk-alogue
diaries delivered with reckless abandon…
dropping your Mach-o, Mach-o Man 'tool
belt' to the floor and, hey dude, somebody's
vulnerability's showing: you're flashing
titillating glimpses of psyche, the temperature's
rising, and everybody's getting a liberal mind's-
eyeful of your blushing soul *au naturel*… but
that's what poetry is, *isn't* it: a personal,

but no-longer-private *peep* show—
Tonight: Real Live (spiritually) Naked Poets!
and you're thinking, *Hell man, they're digging
this… they're wondering just how far you're gonna
go and, well…* even you don't know *that* yet, as
your frantic fingers fumble your life's pages
like buttons and zippers to expose whatever feels
right for this time… this place… this crowd, and…
How many poems did they say I could read?

HEARTBREAK HOTEL

I am the Carlsbad Caverns
emptydark
voluminous

I am the Petrified Forest
pricklybrittle
sterile

I am the Badlands
the Waste Lands
Misery Gore

Dry Gulch
Death Valley
the Hole in the Wall

No Man's Land
the Doldrums
Three Mile Island

Boot Hill
the River Styx and
Dead Man's Curve

Today I am Lake Wobegon
Desolation Row and
the Tallahatchie Bridge…

Tonight I'll be a walk down
Lonely Street. Hell, I'll be the
goddamn Heartbreak Hotel…

HIGH PLAINS DRIFTER

On my faithful steed, the green-and-cream
Columbia one-speed who answers to Trigger,
I cowboy up Pleasant Street at a gallop
on one of those early-spring late afternoons...
temperature sundowning south of freezing,
the icy wind chill feathering my hair, my
bare knuckles and ears white with impending
frostbite, and my spring jacket unzipped...
snapping like a leather vest in the breeze
> *(ever see Roy Rogers riding all buttoned*
> *up to the neck in three layers or*
> *wearing mittens for <u>his</u> mom...?)*
to whoa-up under the low naked limbs of
the playground maples, inching to a dead stop,
feet still on the pedals... upright... balanced...
(trick rider that I am) *(Easy, fella...)* and slowly,
eversocareful... standing upright... poised
precariously in the stirrups
> *(to the thunder of the*
> *rodeo crowd applause!)*
and reach up to pluck the first of the
finger fruit from the lowest branch, a long,
sap-sweetencd, icicle flecked with bits of
black bark... clamping it in my teeth like
a Longbranch cheroot,
my tongue delighting itself
along the maple-ish
Swishersweet surface...

me
a big forerunner of
the Marlboro Man.

HOMBRE

With no real shot glasses
in The House That Never Drinks
or Smokes or Swears...

I bartender my own grape juice
into the tiniest, most-shotglass-*like*
juice glass in the cupboard—

Pour me a stiff one, Tommy me boy...
just a coupla fingers on the bottom
if you don't mind...

and toss it back with a leathery
Richard Widmark grimace—
"Aaaaahh..."

and drop down off the barstool... thumbs
hooked in my creaking gunbelt... the
wooden match drooping rakishly

from my Tombstone poker face...
and push my way through the
batwing doors

to step out into the street
in the OK Corral sunshine
to see who's

calling me out *this* time...
and *Ol' Hoss, they just*
never learn, do *they!*

I, ROBOT

I sing my body electric… state-of-the-art
luxury sports utility vehicle of the species!
Nothing like me ever was! Built like a
brick shit house to last, to take a licking
and keep on ticking…

Modeled on the redundancy principle—
extra brain hemisphere, superfluous kidney,
lung, eye, hand, foot, and five senses, each
with its software-bundled hardware connected
by spaghetti-tangles of fiber-optic nerves to

the mother of all boards! Every cell vacuum-packed
with its own copy of the spiro-encrypted, double-
helixed, micro-schematic blueprint, and every digit
stamped with its encrypted
swirl-pattern 'scan code'!

Oh, I'm the quintessential, self-replicating,
self-healing, self-cleaning, psycho-medical
chemico-robotic Circuit City wonder— drop
me on an alien planet and *watch*: at one-tenth
brain capacity, I'll invent the wheel, steal fire

from the Titans, change the water into wine,
clone myself, and when there's enough of
me and enough time and typewriters…
we will compose
Hamlet!

IMITATION OF LIFE

When I went to the movies alone
I could weep in the darkness
when they put Ol' Yeller down…
or when the little blonde kid
wailed *Shane! Shane!* while Shane
rode stupidly off into the credits…

When I went to the movies alone
it was almost *Holy* like in church,
like worshipping creation on the screen
(the creation of someone *accessible*)
each film being another chapter
in a Bible even *I* could read…

When I went to the movies alone
it was like being in school, only a
real school that only taught Life 101—
all the stuff you really needed to know
but were afraid to ask, all the stuff
they never had the guts to tell you…

When I went to the movies alone
I learned how to go out in a blaze of
glory, when to ride off into the sunset,
how to get Natalie Wood to fall
for me by the end of the show—
that you put girls on pedestals…

Sure, I'd sit with my brother when he went…
or Freddie, my cousin… Jerry or Steve…
but it was always so much more…
spiritual
when I did *that*
when I went to the movies alone…

IT

In yesteryear's B-horror movies, it was usually
the hapless custodian who 'bought the farm' first,
routinely sweeping up the midnight floors of the
Secret Government Nuclear Testing Facility...
or the mad scientist's lab... or the morgue...
suddenly becoming aware that the sealed door

to *The Restricted Area* is yawning inexplicably *ajar,*
and then being drawn to just stand there before it...
puzzled and teetering on responsibility's fence:
I should report this immediately... but inevitably
leaning into that one little, that let's-just-make-
sure-first *look-see...* and all of us in the peanut

gallery *praying* in mute hysteria, *Jiminy Crickets!*
don't... open...that... Oh, the horror! The horror!
But then of course... well, he *was,* after all, only
a nameless stereotype... just a *janitor...* probably
didn't have a life anyway... (see, I was a kid then)

So how'd I get here, balding, salt and pepper in
my beard, pushing this broom down these dark
creepy corridors and almost *positive* I just heard...
something *moving...* behind that locked door
(at least, it's *supposed* to be locked)... *Uhmmm...*
Hello??? Anybody... there...?

IT HAPPENS EVERY SPRING

> *Rin Tin Tin*
> *swallowed a pin…*
> *went to the doctor*
> *but the doctor wasn't in!*

Two rising and falling playground pistons
flouncing pigtails and ponytails between
a pair of stoically chanting sisters
cranking the jump rope
weaving the jump rope
into a blurred cocoon
between the snow windrows
and mud puddles…

> *Opened the door*
> *fell on the floor*
> *and that was the end*
> *of Rin Tin Tin!*

and the flock of mothers' little kerchiefed-
daughters, sweater-breasted, mitten-winged
recess sparrows ringing 'round the recess
ritual of early spring

> *in comes the doctor!*
> *in comes the nurse!*
> *in comes the lady with*
> *the big fat purse!*

and somebody cackles
Salt and pepper! and
the cadence accelerates:

> *Outgoesthedoctor!Outgoesthenurse!*
> *Outgoestheladywiththebigfatpurse!*

JAWS   (to Officer Brody...)

We're gonna need a bigger boat... is what I say to Phyl... us, surrounded by the circus of breaching leviathans, fantails wider than the *Orca's* deck on this whale watch I swore she'd never drag *me* on after twice reading *Moby Dick* and watching *Jaws* a few too many times (if that's possible)... her seeing me as The Clown, my familiar humor only a fleeting distraction— my sole purpose on earth: keeping this woman in smiles— but me, seriously identifying with *Jaw's* hydrophobic Brody, weak in the knees with vertigo at the thought of twenty thousand leagues of watery grave looming below us and patiently trolling the surface... waiting on Ol' Man Gravity to reel us down... so, humor being my best coping skill, like whistling through the cemetery at midnight, I kill both gulls with one stone, leaning into her as we brace for the next swell on our rubbery sea legs, and plucking the invisible Chesterfield out of my mug and crushing it under the toe of my boat shoe while muttering in my best Bogart...

When this tub goes belly-up, kid, shtick with me, see? I got us a plan. "And what's the big plan, Ahab?" *Party balloons, shweetheart...* "Party balloons?" *That's right, beautiful: I'm packin'— The way I see it, when this floating coffin rolls over, I give you half, see? That's when we start blowin' em up 'n stuffin' our shirts...*

But sudden flukes slap surf off the starboard and I lose her to the spectacle— so I too marvel for a while... secretly fingering that very real packet of red, green, yellow and blue birthday balloons nesting in my jacket pocket!

JURASSIC PARK

Like those embedded-in-amber
mosquitoes whose blood-bloated
bellies gave up the ingested ghosts
of DNA to populate *Jurassic Park*
with long-gone, born-again
Thunder Lizards…

my poems, like moths fluttering
in the widescreen's glow, glue
themselves into the fly-paper of
the world wide web, their tiny little
torsos mummifying, crystallizing
into the jaundiced jewelry of time…

waiting for *you* to stumble on them
and, perhaps, reconstruct a Paleozoic
portrait, if you will, in the museum
of your heart… of your head… a
hologram of a *soul* that once
walked this earth

LITTLE BIG MAN

When beer-bellied Drill Instructor Minton
barks, "Ok all yew little low-life sum-bitches:
on your *feet!*" every stiff-starched recruit
pops *to* like toast from the mess hall toaster...

the exception being this day-dreaming half-pint
with 'Rogers' stenciled across his breast, still
chewing pensively on a stalk of grass and
whatever private thoughts a five-foot private may

entertain while sprawled idyllically on the lawn
even as death in his Smokey the Bear hat bears
down, eclipsing the sun and possibly his future.
"S'mattuh, boy? yew deaf or sumpin'?" Bravo

Company's interest in the lethal silence goes all
keen and *prurient*... *"No, I heard you, Drill
Sergeant..."* Minton's face twitches now; this, a
moment D.I.'s *live* for, a D.I.'s *wet dream*...

"So jus' whut iz yore sorry-ass 'scuse *then,
Buzzard-bait?"* (on *Wild Kingdom* this would
be just before the leopard hamstrings the gazelle
and drags it down kicking as the camera pans

discreetly away). Private Rogers takes us
all in with a sweep of his hand... *"Far as I
can tell, Drill Sergeant, all the little low-life
'sum-bitches' are <u>on</u> their feet..."*

After lights-out, I still lie here on my bunk
listening to our lone little big man out there
circling and circling B-company's barracks
at double-time… in the rain… the fifty-pound

pack strapped to his back…
rifle raised over his head… and
(you gotta admit it: the boy's got heart!)
belting it right out:

> *"I'm a little low-life suh-hum bih-hitch!"*
> *"I'm a little low-life suh-hum bih-hitch!"*

THE LOST WEEKEND

A puppet on somebody else's strings,
but longing to be a real live boy, I
told my long-nosed lies, conned my
fairy godmother and, before you knew
it, was a half-assed fugitive running
from the lights and delights of

Pleasure Island... Lying low, I
took me a room at The Belly of the
Whale Inn and began playing a
waiting game with Time... but
Time never gives an inch, and all
I won was a bad case of the

rock-bottom-blues bends so bad,
I bobbed up under the stark sun
like a bone dry champagne cork...
later coming to strapped to a bed
in the... *decompression* ward?
(...or the de-*something* ward)

THE LOST WORLD

You took it for granted …
just *assumed* Memory Lane
would forever remain
your Yellow Brick Road

overlooking, way back then, those
sleepy seeds borne on the winds of
time, sowing themselves in between
the cobblestones, and then…

all those little spearheads, the crabgrass
unsheathing itself up underfoot, choking
the undergrowth of Memory Lane in
an overgrowth primeval… and now

you've gone missing in the outback of your
own hardening cerebral arteries… all your
Hansel and Gretel breadcrumbs disappearing
like hourglass-sand down the little rabbit holes

and you, needing a damn machete to hack
your way in circles through the foliage of
your own life's back pages… unable to find
even the forest hiding behind the trees…

THE MATING GAME

Back when The Nightlife meant
rec center, a basketball game, or
a double-feature sandwiched
between the curfews and chores
and the high school gossip-rag
headlines… back when all it took
to play the game was a little dab
of Brylcreem, a good set of
wheels, and a class ring… when
the wages of sin were dickies
to hide the hickies,
or a bad case of
blue-balls blues…

You taller virgin Bambi girls,
with your two-year jumpstart on
armpit-hair maturity, were the
musical chairs round and round which
we ready-or-not hormonal colts pranced
to "The Flight of the Bumblebee"…
making out, and breaking up with us…
grinding our hearts to hamburger…
leaving us to drown our sorrows
in those lonely loved 'n lost lyrics
that sang us head-over-heels into,
and back out of, the have-a-heart
traps of lustlove…

MEMPHIS BELLE

Head in the Hollywood clouds,
my wet-behind-the-ears license in
wallet, I taxi the old Pontiac down
the driveway and lumber out onto
Pleasant Street… fondling the stick,
and then gunning that Flying Fortress
up to speed, and droning off into a
wild blue yonder on the tiny tailwind
of my one-windsock-town life,

flying my freelance recon missions…
deftly yawing to the right of
those evenly spaced yellow
'tracers' zinging back at me
up the middle of my personal
highway to hell and back, the
soul-jarring thunder-flak of
the potholes jarring the
warbird's underbelly…

and then barnstorming
the wide sweeping curve
to that truss-bridge target
way-the-hell-and-gone
down there at the bottom of
the valley and then buzz-
cutting straight through it,
and scrambling all those Nazi
pigeons from here to eternity!

THE MIRACLE WORKER

Rummage-sale Saturday! Excitement so thick you can stir it with a spoon! Blue-haired little old ladies: Nanny and Lottie and Edie, as fragrant as wilted lilacs, already on board, the front passenger door yawning open like the black jawbone of Noah's whale, all waiting on Aunt Sadie— Mom at the wheel and me in the back seat, crooked elbow poked out the window, arm hugging the window-frame post, those fresh buffalo nickels burning holes in my pocket, me dreaming of a new-used 10¢ jigsaw puzzle with no more than a couple pieces missing and '*Dance With Me Henry*' be-bopping the radio, my visions of hand-me-down sugarplums dancing to the beat... and me oblivious to feeble Sadie's eighty-two pounds now daintily settling into the front seat, until... *she slams her door on my hand* and all hell breaks loose, a shrill squeal piping out of me like steam from the teakettle left on the stove, and me flipping around like a hooked sunfish on the bottom of a boat, but through the electric pain and the sirens screaming in my head, Sadie's barking something up front there, but not *moving...* and not opening the *door*, no... but wait: she's praying to God I think (but *not* opening her door) and the pandemonium's like a cage of panicked parakeets where nobody's able to even guess *what* to do— but suddenly Mom's here, yanking the door open, freeing my rat-trapped pinkies and commanding, *Wiggle your fingers! Wiggle your fingers!* and I *do...* Mom announcing, *He's all right! They're not broken!* and Sadie hoarsely crowing...

    Puh-raise the Lord! It's a miracle!

NIGHT OF THE LIVING DEAD

My spirit finally crashed like the
Black Sunday stock market... all
my futures swimming belly-up and my
soul flushing for the third and final spiral
down the plumbing of my great depression...

and long after the dark waters receded, all
that was left: this morally bankrupt, driftwood
mummy... bleached *beach trash*... a parched,
and desiccated husk with a papery wasp-nest
heart, a parchment bellows for lungs, and

a couple of cringing, hysterical
prisoner-of-war *eyes* looking
out the little bunker slot
between the head bandages...
a non-entity...

the 'un-dead'...
a certifiable, flat-lining,
catacomb *casket*-case,
the creature who walks among us
shuffling down eternity boulevard

remembering (academically) that
laughter's the best medicine!
but unable to cough up
a laugh to save
my life...

NORTH TO ALASKA

The spring playground, muddy as a main street
from the forgotten Klondike Goldrush, peopled
with forty little Dangerous Dan McGrews—
hell-bent, big-time wannabe-gamblers all—
cow-licked hustlers, rubes in little suspenders
beneath mothball-fresh spring jackets...

some pirouetting spastically on the heels of their
galoshes, gouging casino craters out of the wet,
spring gravel, and each with his pinchable poke of
precious nuggets: cats-eyes and clearies, aggies,
swirls, double-centers, steelies, and moonstones...
most bragging manfully of past conquests and

bankrupted foes, speculating on jackpot futures of
marble millions— first a little game of 'funsies'
to draw in the crowd, and then 'keepsies'
to separate the men from the boys,
and then the boys from the marbles...
and there's a sucker born every minute...

OCTOBER SKY

In PJ's we pad over dewy grass in the October chill
to mount the '48 Plymouth lying like a cold black
boulder under the star-studded nightvelvet sky
(me on the roof—on my back) and we're early,

so it's like the drive-in movies, dark enough for the
impatient horns to start honking. Only we're not out
here for a comedy or cowboy flick, but something
dark, something sci-fi, something Flash Gordonish

because nothing but the Aurora Borealis, a random
meteor, or the blinking beacon of your occasional
prop-driven airliner *ever* moves up there in our
nightsky… and so we fidget, waiting on that corner

of heaven we've been warned to watch…
whispering in hushed reverence and consulting
the big radium-dial Dad keeps in his pocket
when: *There it is! There! Right there! See it!?*

The first untwinkling 'star' *ever*
swimming across The Big Dipper,
plotting a geometrically-precise
straight line and clocking a faster

transit of the firmament than
any four-engine TWA— stunned
with awe, we quietly mouth
the holy word…

Sputnik!

ON GOLDEN POND

Head-over-heels in love with
love, we imagined our primping
reflections as Avalon and Funicello
memorizing our lines in the mirror
for the Big Screen Tests of Dating,
the Auditions of Going Steady...

Me scouting out a Sandra Dee to
play opposite my Troy Donahue, you
issuing a casting call for a handsome
Hudson for your Doris Day... but it
wasn't Hollywood— a collaborative
compromise was in order...

Our co-starring debut would be
The American Dream
the serio-comic heartthrob
starring the matinee idols,
us! We inked the
contracts on location...

And today, with
The Big Chill far behind us,
we've got one more feature left...
our grand finale, this dream-team's
very own *On Golden Pond*—
a shoo-in for the Oscars...

OUR TOWN

In the museum of the skull, the reruns
loop endlessly like old *Twilight Zone*
episodes shuffled into the pages of
To Kill a Mockingbird— the Andy and
Opie Main Street of Webber's Hardware,
Merrick Square Market, Center Theater…
and Lanpher's Drug Store, the churches,
the county jail and parsonage, the school
playground with its slide and swings…
and that dark, dead house on School Street
shunned and haunted by its own urban legend…

And the usual suspects, of course; the cast of
characters who strolled through your forever-
unlocked doors: the milkman and iceman in the
kitchen, the postman and paperboy in the hallway,
the bedside doctor who felt your forehead, the
sleazy insurance agent in the Panama hat who just
popped in without knocking and helped himself to
the premium envelope hanging on *his* kitchen
wall-hook, side-by-side with our house keys…
and then just down the street: our very own
'Boo Radley,' and that wizened old crone

who berated you from her witch's wicker
porch rocker because you were guilty of being
young, and she knew your name, and more about
your father than you ever would… that gossip
who tapped into everything you ever whispered
over your five-party line…

The neighborhood… just a footnote now

PETER PAN

When I was ten (back when the
Sunday-School purpose-of-life was
never to tell a lie and to think only
pure thoughts) I could never dig what
Popeye saw in librarian-plain Olive Oyl...
what was keeping *me* up nights was

the little independent movie theater
in my head, featuring all those jailbait
Disney girls of Peter Pan, those Mermaids
of Marooner's Rock, the real reason for
flying into Neverland for the weekend...
scantily-clad and always happy to see you,

the Island Girls' Welcoming and Entertainment
Committee for lost boys looking for a bit of
R-and-R... sweet, petite Tinkerbell, pouty and
deliciously jealous in that hot little jungle-green
number, and those legs... Mr. Disney, what were
you thinking? I might not choose to swing on a

star but hey, carry 'moonbeams' home in a jar...
back to my room? And of course Wendy, my first
pin-up, gliding around night and day in little more
than her modest and sexy powder-blue nightgown
and slippers... more than willing to play house,
darn your socks, sew your shadow back on...

PINOCCHIO

Did the virgin-pure, see-no-evil
hearts of any of those *other* little boys
in the flickery moviedark leap up
(like mine) at all of those all-night,
carnie-barker come-ons amid the
sparkleworks of Pleasure Island…

those Big Rock Candy Mountain
free cigars… that stained-glass
church window just begging you
to pitch a brick through it… that
punch-somebody-in-the-face-and-
get-away-with-it 'rough house'…

or those mugs of draft beer at the
Pleasure Island Pool Hall Emporium?
Did the no-curfew concept also set
their y-chromosomes resonating like
little tuning forks in the dark?
Did *Pinocchio* arouse the

snakes and snails and puppy
dog tails in those guys too?
Or (*Good Lord!*) was I
the only donkey boy
in that
crowd?

RADIOACTIVE DREAMS

A wooden stake to the heart, or the sun's rays, will kill a vampire...

I favored the *sun*— less risky than pinning those
Nosferatu arms down while keeping the stake
perpendicular (I couldn't drive a nail into a *cheese*
log!) and anyway, vampires back then were such
a gullible lot, so easily tricked into staying out just
past dawn and then... *just throw open the shutters!*

But by seventh grade, after *On the Beach*
came and went, the ol' *'sunrise surprise'*
wasn't *just* for vampires anymore, not when a
ground-zero fireball could pop you like bag of
Orville Redenbacher's, smoke you like a Pall Mall,
melt you like a marshmallow on a stick, like some

Count Dracula in the Transylvanian sunshine—
yeah, *a high dose of Roentgens makes Jack a dull
boy*, as listless as those pale Victorian beauties in
their sexy white negligees, sick abed and preyed
upon by the ghastly moonlight visitor— only *not*
pale or prurient, *your* skin would bubble-blister

scalding red, and your hair would comb out in
clumps, your bones turn kindling-brittle, your
teeth tumble out and roll like dice over your
tongue, your fever boil the blood from a turnip,
and you'd dehydrate and mummify with the
vomiting and stomach cramps and diarrhea—

Not very Hollywood, eh? No, not a very sports-
manlike adversary at all… and so it paid to learn
how many inches of lead, and how many feet of
concrete would shield the rays… that even shelves
loaded with books would block *some* gammas, that
radiation travels in straight lines so your air ducts

must be crooked, and capped with tin cones, and
camouflaged in the rosebushes or inside a hollow
tree because (as *The Twilight Zone* taught us all)
Frankenstein's torch-wielding mob will pound
down your door screaming, *never mind me
but for god's sake: take my* baby*!!!*

So day after day I'd pedal my bike, peddling
my Cold War headlines from porch to porch,
and in my head, worry out the blueprints for
my fallout shelter, picking out the bookshelf
titles and calculating how much food and water…
and approximately how many shotgun shells…

REBEL WITHOUT A CAUSE   (for Scotty)

You could usually be found in your
steel-toe engineer boots, fearing no
evil down in the valley of the shadows
under the marquee's dying red neon
reflecting off the bumper-hubcap
chrome of somebody's low-slung
Merc' with the windows cracked and
The Crystals belting out your
personal soundtrack... *He's a rebel
and he'll never be... any good...*

You manning the night, our graveyard-shift
sidewalk superintendent, the grim midnight
crossing-guard... our small-town cross
between James Dean and Brando with a little
James Coburn sprinkled around that toothpick or
Lucky poking out the corner of your rugged mug
and '*BORN TO LOSE*' tattooed blue like a bruise
on the back of your wrist... and we half-pint,
shrimp-boat wannabe street-urchins hanging pilot-
fish close when the bullies put the pressure on

because belying all that bad-assss badness
was a scarred and tarnished-white knight
willing (for some reason) to champion the
justice of us little guys and underdogs
looking up to you through your
crummy self-esteem and
wishing that we too,
like you, could
somehow be...
born to lose

REEFER MADNESS

Once upon a time in the late 40's…
shortly after I began cutting teeth…
the nursery became, all of a sudden,
baby's first opium den— Mom
still marvels how I stopped crying
and dropped right off to sleep
just like that after massaging a dollop
of her favorite over-the-counter opiate

into the tender and swollen teething sores
of my five-month-old gummy-gum-gums.
Paregoric: the mom's best friend, a product
that really worked for once— and my brain
(no dummy, even then) as eager to learn
as any Pavlovian dog, coming alive with
messages flashing in and among the
synapses: *Brain to gums… brain to gums,*

come in please... Roger, brain, this is gums,
go ahead, brain— *Ten-four, gums. That last dose*
was a beaut… whatever you do, just keep'em
coming— you copy? Roger wilco that, brain—
over and out... yes, message received: laugh
and the world laughs with you… cry, and you cry
and get stoned… I like to imagine my cunning little
self swaddled in a powder-blue security blanket

and *jonesing* for my next fix! Wonder if I
snored like a banshee as a little babe coked
to the gills... bet I did a lot of gratuitous 'crying'...
Hell… I'd have cut extra teeth if I *could'*ve!

REQUIEM

Up against the wall of my womb I was already
grooving to someone's kitchen radio *out there*
playing *I've Got You Under My Skin*... and
at five, my twin-sister cousins already had me
be-bopping to *Dance With Me Henry*...

and on one seventh-grade summer night, I first
steered a summering city girl 'round the roller
rink as the Danleers crooned *One Summer Night*...
I smoked my first cigarette singing
Smoke Gets in Your Eyes and, like you,

cut my guitar-pickin' teeth on
The House of the Rising Sun... enrolled
in college on *The Eve of Destruction*...
graduated *To Sir With Love*... and then
soundtracked all the rest of my days to

the likes of Billy Joel, Dr. Hook, Harry
Chapin, Johnny Cash and Elton John... so
hey, when *I* pass? Play some things *I'd* like,
OK? Really *make* a joyful noise for once,
why don't you? Give me a jukebox funeral...

THE RIGHT STUFF

Fifty years ago, when all the psychological test
results were finally in, the scientific intelligentsia
pontificated: man will never— *can* never—
travel the measureless emptiness…
survive the stark *loneliness* of

the big-bang to the stars, so hopelessly
social is his nature, so utterly dependent
is he upon human warmth, upon *real* contact
with his village
with his tribe

But today, a generation of innerspace-astronaut
sons and daughters and nieces and nephews
with uncanny hand-eye-mouse coordination,
self-strapped into the consoles of wireless
suspended animation in their space-capsule

bedrooms, have launched their cargo-lives on
drifting trajectories through the days, months and
years of cyber-space… utterly *alone*… but chatting
endlessly in virtual chat rooms in virtual bliss,
resolving virtual conflicts with virtual combat,

developing virtual relationships, leading
steamy virtual sex lives, and leaving us
behind… their baby-boomer elders…
tethered back here on terra firma
by our own virtual umbilicals…

THE RIVER OF NO RETURN

Mama said, *Whatever you do, just stay away*
from the river… so I became Tom Sawyer
and made the Piscataquis my Mississippi
where we'd fish from small boulders and
fall in every day, trying to float that old

door as a raft poled by broomsticks, just like
Fess Parker and Buddy Ebsen in the movie
Davy Crockett and the River Pirates— and
we'd haunt the old off-limits Indian cave
where some kid fell off a ledge and died

the year before, us believing we'd find
arrowheads and maybe his ghost, but
finding only graffiti… and after watching
Spencer Tracy and Robert Wagner rappel
down those sheer rock faces in *The Mountain,*

we scurried over to Nat's dad's garage for a coil
of rope, climbed up on the river's highest ledge,
and tied one end 'round a tree trunk… me going
first 'cause the squeaky wheel gets the grease…
only smoking rope-burns blistered my palms

and the fall to that rock-bottomed river bed
practically fractured my kneecaps… but I
had to keep all that secret because Mama
said, *Whatever you do, just stay away*
from the river…

SENTIMENTAL JOURNEY

The screen door slams and the headlines
cry *Ike!* and *Ted Williams!* while the
Philco way in the back cranks out
'The Ballad of a Teenage Queen.'
My Red Ball Jets pad reverently
over the oil-darkened hardwood past
the register's *ka-ching*-promise of
Indian head pennies in your change,
down the aisle of warped shelving
stacked like the Walls of Jericho...
the Prince Macaroni boxes elbowing
the Campbell Soup cans... through
the ripe-banana, apple-onion
medley with its pungent tang of
white cheddar from the big
cheesewheel-under-glass...

past glass-bottled, fresh, white milk chilling
in the refrigerated window display, bottle-capped
with collectable, redeemable, half-dollar-size
cardboard discs... and on down to the back where
sea-glass green coke bottles languish like lobsters
neck-deep in the ice water of the open-top
fire-engine-red holding tank beneath the
fading, once festive Fanta, Fudgesicle, Moxie
and Necco signs... and all those dangling
amber banana-curls of slime-gummy
fly-paper, the houseflies raisin-glued
above the jaundiced jars of pickled eggs,
pickled spiced sausages, and those
wax-papered Italians stacked
atop the meat counter
calling my name—

A SHOT IN THE DARK

Today it's a 'theft of services'... but back then,
back when we were all twelve-year-old 'patrons
of the arts,' sneaking into the movies seemed a
relatively innocent necessity, what with the price
of admission skyrocketed to 35¢ and security being
hair-trigger taut in those desperate times: the mens'
room window in lockdown, the backdoor exit under
constant scrutiny, Tilly the ticket-taker stationed
strategically down at the end of the
velvet-roped lobby and Ivan 'the Terrible,'
proprietor, propped back Wild Bill Hickok-style
in his open-door-office chair, waiting in ambush
for any dastardly movie-rustlers, like ourselves...

And who came up with it... *the plan?* Each of us
laying his scavenged silver in the palm of that day's
designated Billy the Kid who, with his wildest
war-whoop, ran zigging around the ticket booth,
zagging past Tilly, hoo-hooting down into the
tilted-floor darkness with the two-man posse in hot
pursuit, and us unseen on their heels, disappearing
like Apaches into the shadows... and then, from
ill-gotten seats, watching the *real* show: our own
Ol' Billy Boy sweet-talking his captors, assuring
them that, oh by golly, he'd had the money all
along, this just being all a big joke you know,
all in fun— *See: look here: here's the 35¢!*

And them swallowing this hook, line, and sinker—
Well, ok this *time, but...!* And then patting
themselves on the back for being so
quick on the draw and all...
and always getting their man.

THE SILENCE OF THE LAMBS

Yes, a sleep apneac, a bona-fide
Registered Sleep Offender, condemned
for snoring snores that march to a different,
louder drum— now, life-sentenced
nightly, my head saddle-cinched tightly

in hellish Halloweenish headgear—
my handsome face a mockery now...
me, the Man in the Iron Mask chained
to the nightstand by the garden hose
connected to the creepy black-box

technology malevolently humming
on the nightstand, maintaining my
beachball-inflated skull at 32 pounds
per square inch... and me, rolling
cumbersomely wifeward, trying for a

serious *I love you* despite the hapless Hannibal
Lecter leer... *Can you hear the lambs, Clarisse?*
Gigglesnorting my nose-gear loose
and setting off a sibilant *pppsssshhh!*
(an air-leak pissing off the starboard)

and me clawing at my face, blind in the scuba
darkness and needing my buddy-system partner
to slap her own breathing apparatus over my
nose, to rescue me in the sheets so we can
ascend to the rising sun of morning together...

SPELLBOUND

The *real* black magic of my youth? The music
from the 'phonograph,' the medium of the séance…
lights all lowered for atmosphere, the campy
ember-burn of the vacuum tubes casting their
gypsy candleglow upon the wall behind… and

me, sitting there in the dark all by my little
lonesome, letting the instruments and voices
snake-charm me down into those midnight
grooves right into someone else's jealousy…
letting them conjure up in me somebody

else's pain and blues… letting them possess me
with someone else's yearning… and then, well…
I'd find myself in somebody else's skin… in
somebody else's emotional blue suede shoes…
in somebody else…

so yeah, small fry
though I was, it was
me giving Peggy Lee that
Fe-ver… in the morning, yeah…
fever all through the night…

SPLENDOR IN THE GRASS

No,
we are *not*
marking our territory
as the sociologists insist…
it is only to atone for our
Herculean, snakes-and-snails-
and-puppy-dog-tails' *sins* that
we men eternally mow our lawns
in the blistering, blackfly-infested
gamma rays of the sun
all of our days… back lawns
upon which almost no one
ever walks, back lawns
that few ever glimpse…

It is a test from the same
gods who dared Oedipus,
Sure, try escaping your fate…
see what happens…
go ahead—
make our day…
gods that appear today
as *wives*…

No,
tell the sociologists
that we are marking
our *wives'*
territories

STAR WARS

It helps to think of life as a movie— in fact:
make life *your* movie... life imitates art imitates
life, after all, and no matter how relatively boring
or exciting or noir you find *your* soap opera,
it's still your basic adventure with the same
old textbook conflicts, crises, climaxes,
and final resolutions—

In my 'movie,' I start out as a
Redneck every bit as insignificant
As Luke Skywalker was at first...
he, the backwater, desert-planet
farm boy lusting for something
a lot more cliffhanger-romantic...
Watch what you pray for!

There's a Rebel Alliance in my story too,
along with an Evil Empire, if you will,
and even a 'Death Star' of sorts (if you're
willing to stretch a metaphor)... that darkside,
black-hole *influence* out there, just over
the forbidden-fruit event horizon, posted:
Life really sucks beyond this point!

And then you'll find that Real Life has its
own colorful cast of characters too, plenty of
Greedos and Jabba the Hutts to go around— but
if you can just make that jump to light speed,
just star-hop through the trust barrier, you'll find
legions of R2D2's, C3PO's and Chewbaccas...
and even the occasional Obi-wan Kenobe

THE STING

I love the little *pick-me-up*
of a slap-splash of aftershave
on my nicked neck…

of iodine seeping into the fresh
cat-scratch: the surge, the crescendo
the climax of the biting sting…

Such a relief!

I'm like the tongue that discovers
the newly-chipped, razor-sharp
cuspid… and then throws itself on it

like some blood-swollen breaker
lashing the coral reefs at
full-moon high tide

repeatedly, endlessly
mercilessly,
for *days*…

so go ahead…
rub a little salt
in my wound

SWEET AND LOWDOWN

Give me Sandburg praising Chicago,
City of the Big Shoulders, Hog Butcher
for the World; give me Baraka's
Preface to a Twenty Volume Suicide Note,
Bukowsky's *Last Night of the Earth...*

Play me the sour-sung dirges of
smoke-filled bars, sing me Joplin's
raspy '*Half Moon*' and growl those
long-gone, down-on-the-dirt-floor-
cellar rants of Tom Waits...

And while I'm at it, don't be
putting any goddamn strawberries
in my rhubarb pie— like to sweeten
the poetry right out of 'em! I like
my eloquence straight up and tart!

TARZAN AND HIS MATE

me negative— you positive
me alphabetic— you numeric
me dog in last life— you probably *daffodil*
me make *idea*— you make quilt
me? AMC mean *American Movie Classics*
you? it mean *All My Children*
me like Tarantino— you like chick-flick
me hairy— you smooth
me Tarzan— you Jane

you *do*— me *think*
you happy camper— me hate mosquitoes
you dream home and garden— me just *nap*
you like Red Sox— me like poet laureates
your computer? humongous embroidery machine
my computer? heap-big juke box
you always too busy— me learn say *no* real quick
you snore— OK, me snore too (a little)
you Jane— me Tarzan

THE THREE MUSKETEERS

Oh, the fun we had… we Three Musketeers
(minus two)
sitting around those Salem - Kool - Marlboro
'campfires' all island-cozy… spouting
soliloquies…mouthing monologues…

and what about all those crazy songs we sang
why, we were practically the Kingston Trio
(minus two)
like 'Only the Lonely' or
'The Last Word in Lonesome Is Me'

'So Lonesome I Could Cry'…
and oh, the *games* we played,
we Three Horsemen of Apocalypse
(minus two)
like... Monk in the Monastery...

Lone Lighthouse Keeper…
Fire Tower Man...
Robinson Crusoe…
Last Man on Earth…
and oh yes,

Solitaire
Lots of Solitaire
me, myself, and I
(all three of us)
The fun we had!

THUNDER ROAD

Let me tell the story,
I can tell it all
about the mountain boy
who ran illegal alcohol

A twelve-year-old Walter Mitty,
I got 'older' after *Thunder Road*
left the movie theater and me
in its black and white dust... hung
up my neverneverland shadow and
got in touch with the darker side of
getaway-car noir... contemplated a
future of rum-running Kentucky
moonshine, of outrunning the
revenuers and rival bootleggers
over moonlit mountain roads...

His daddy made the whiskey,
the son, he drove the load
and when his engine roared they
called the highway thunder road!

and in the bathroom mirror,
honed my best 'Bob Mitchum,'
practicing his sleepy bar-room
eyes and willing the cleft in *his*
jaw into my own undimpled chin,
talking tough with the wooden
'Pall Mall' match glued to my wry
grimace, and logging hours languishing
behind the big wheel of that black
rusting derelict out behind the barn
exuding its mild halitosis of mold,

mildew, iron oxide and sun-rotted
tire rubber... the witchgrass grown
right up between the manifold and
floorboards— me, elevated on
a stack of pillows gone A.W.O.L.
from the living room sofa...
right hand on the wheel, left
elbow crooked out the window:
Mr. Cool...
Mr. Nonchalance...
Mr. Bob Mitchum because...

> *when my engine*
> *roars they call*
> *the highway*
> *Thunder Road*

THE TROJAN WOMEN

We were the wee warrior-prince knights of
the round ball, ambassadors of sportsmanship
departing in dress slacks and white shirts,
clip-on neckties and Sunday shoes, our
superegos zipped away in duffle bags…

sailing off with drumbeat hearts aboard yellow
schoolbus ships bound for the exotic kingdoms
of Brownville… or East Millinocket… honoring
our flag in combat, entering arenas to Trojan War
roars in the maroon and white dazzle of our
livery…

and the damsels, their cheerleaders… sirens of
bewitching beauty, each bevy containing at least
one face to launch a thousand school buses…
the Helen of that night's Troy… and each of us
a horny, hopeful, preadolescent Paris privately

fantasizing her abduction, lustfully spiriting
her away in our hearts and onto the school bus
to flee back across the home borders to some
impossible-to-imagine happy-ever-after… but
later, alas, under the same old winter moon,

only one of us or, at most two, clutching the
prize… a hastily lip-sticked phone number
on a folded napkin, one bright ember
of hope burning bright in the
heart of the bus darkness…

TROY

No Odysseus, me, but a liar-storyteller
of ignoble reputation nonetheless— my
personal Troy, a smoldering smudge
on a horizon four-years-astern on my
wine dark wake and yes, all of my
infamous wooden horses, flung
from the carousel of desperation,
litter the cratered beachhead

No, I did not conquer...
no, I did not succumb... fighting
the fight of the cornered rat,
I *survived*... and there are
no medals, no parades
no Veterans' Days for
cornered-rat
survivors

So perhaps it is appropriate, after all,
to languish out here under the Promethean
sun in The Doldrums: no fuel, busted
compass, torn sail... earplugged and
blindfolded, safe from the Sirens' song—
but missing you, and
waiting for the gods...
or the sharks

TWISTER

I pray for the electricblue *crescendo*
of a jagged, mind-blowing
fuse-popping, spine-severing
80-megaton *thunderclap!*

for the arctic burn of ozone in my
nostrils, and the fuel-injected
adrenalin jumpstarting my
nervous tics and twitches!

Let the turbine wind play Deathmatch-
Frisbee with dish antennae... let the
purpledark beer belly of the storm-sky
spill its guts, dump thunderloads of

cueballs down in torrents to
ricochet off the cars and chase
me like a hunted jackrabbit
down tornado alley—

See, I'm just lying here on the
couch of inaction... the living dead...
my stereo predicting a bad moon rising,
and me really needing a freaking *storm!*

UP IN SMOKE

I was a pushover, OK… and who'd ever blame
me, the impressionable little innocent sitting on
the floor in front of the TV, waiting out the
sitcoms for his favorite commercial to return…
and then… *there she was…* in living black-and-
white, waltzing around in her white high-heel
majorette *boots made for walkin'* on a pair of
shapely gams that'd make Sam Spade stutter…
legs that went all the way up (to the only other
thing she had on) (in *my* mind)… that three-
foot-high pack-of-Old-Golds costume…
(Wolfwhistle!)

And I guess there was no question I was gonna
give smoking a try… her hurdy-gurdy leaving me
longing to ditch my hayseed family values and run
off with her— Oh, *I'd* be her cute little red-coated
bellhop performing tricks… like the very ultra-cool
popping the ol' Zippo cover with a single finger-
snap, *Hey-presto*: the blue-orange finger of flame!
Or blowing smoke rings through smoke rings
through smoke rings… or flaunting that ol'
'French inhale' and then, like some sexy
fire-breathing dragon, releasing the smoke,
seductively from my nostrils' dual exhaust…

Oh, I was gonna be so cool I'd be
fighting the girls off with a broom!

URBAN LEGEND

It was almost practically an honest-to-God *fact*
(all the older cool guys confirmed it) and we could
all recite those well-known anecdotes seething
with *Rebel Without a Cause* wildness, that same
Walk On the Wild Side jazz we were seeking in
all those breathless teen-angst movies
like *Joy Ride...* and *Party Crashers*:

> 'A single aspirin swilled down
> with a mouthful of Coca-Cola
> will render you staggeringly,
> knocked-on-your-ass *drunk!*'

In one 'medicine show' demonstration, an
otherwise normally 'sober' and 'respectable'
older kid rapidly developed outrageously
slurred speech and flopped with histrionic
helplessness on the playground lawn, reduced
to a giggling, gravity-pinned dying cockroach
impaled on its back! See? Proof-*positive*!

So later of course, in the sanctuary of my room,
surreptitiously gulping down the deliciously-illicit
little white pill with that swig of Coke (*which... as
anyone'll tell you, will completely dissolve the steel
spike left in it over night!*) I waited on the magic
for hours... until finally...
absolutely nothing happened!

> Just like that time I washed down
> chokecherries with the cold glass of
> milk everybody *swore* would kill me!

THE USUAL SUSPECTS

Wilford Brimley, preaching on the TV to
his nation of diabetics, is a dead ringer for
a certain suspendered neighbor of mine
beached like a beluga on his deck recliner...

and my mind's-eye meanders off past the Ford
franchise downtown where some wheelin,' dealin'
Darren McGavin cons the vulnerable into sleazy
used-car deals... and then over to the municipal

building where a sardonic Agnes Moorehead
licenses our pickups and puppies... the funeral
home where our resident John Carradine
unctuously gladhands the bereaved... the bakery

where Aunt Bea's Mayberry cakes rule... to the
parked cruiser with its uni-browed Claude Akins
keeping a jaundiced eye peeled for scofflaws... out
past the graveyard, that *Spoon River Anthology*

of Alice Ghostlys and Paul Lyndes, Dick Yorks and
Elizabeth Montgomerys... and finally, further out
by the town landfill where some scowling Lee Van
Cleef muscles the front-end loader's controls, a

crusty old Andy Devine flattens corrugated card-
board under his workboots, a cockeyed Jack Elam
stacks the newsprint, and a wild Strother Martin
endures an ongoing failure to communicate with

the abandoned Frigidaires in his charge— while *I*,
on my way back to the coffeepot for a refill, force
my eyes to compulsively avoid the mirror where,
damned if some squinting, limping, bent, old...

Walter Brennan isn't lurking in
ambush for me behind the glass...

WEEKEND WARRIORS

   "Take a load off, Fanny..."
Tony's guitar leading us in the chorus
and all of us baying it at the moon
   "take a load for free..."
and Henry's hash pipe (or Percy's bong)
making the rounds 'round Charlie Company's
campfire bellowing its volleys of Fourth of July
sparks up through the evergreen boughs to
the one a.m. stars …
   "take a load off, Fanny..."
we happy hippies, legal draft-dodgers
   "and..."
in the perfect disguise: identical
fatigues and field-jackets,
   "and..."
non-regulation-length hair swept
clandestinely under our caps
   "and..."
hiding in plain sight in National Guard armories
and summer trainings out here in the woods…
   "you put the load (you put the load)
   right on me!"

Flames glinting wildly in our saucer-wide pupils
glinting off the empty Colt 45 cans and other dead
soldiers cobblestoning the pine-needled forest
floor... but *boy,* when those blanks I'd
surreptitiously unloaded into the campfire's flames
(seemed a good idea at the time)
Finished 'cooking' and opened fire
zinging sizzling brass shell casings
every which way in sporadic bursts,

ricocheting off hapless "happy campers"
amid hoots and yelps and gales and gales
of laughter— life was warm and wonderful
because it was summer and I was skunk-drunk...
because the Acapulco gold really *was* magical...
because life had become this *M*A*S*H* comedy
where everything I had to say was funny as hell...

and because I didn't have an inkling,
I guess, that I was really just this
annoying pain in the ass...

THE WILD ONE

And I think, *Holy shit!* eyeballing him across the
chemical dependency rehab's registration hubbub—
A freakin'scarecrow! That weather-beaten biker
jacket hanging on those coat-hanger shoulders…

the jaundiced, rain-ravaged snakeskin boots coiled
beneath the unraveling shade of his threadbare
pantlegs (*roadkill* snakeskin, a snakeskin molting its
scales with a pair of pewtery steel-toe glints

hatching their way out through like patches of
mange)… and ink 'bricks' tattooed down one
sallow leathery cheek, disappearing under the
ragged neck of his black T-shirt. Apparently he

what? doesn't have a glass jaw? Maybe he's
The Wild One… or the Robert De Niro from
Taxi Driver (an emaciated De Niro— a De Niro
with A.I.D.S., a hair-trigger, loose cannon De Niro)

and sure enough, right after Nurse Ratched (for
my safety) confiscates my English Leather and
my Listerine… my new roommate comes climbing
back in through the window of *our* cubicle

(*our* new little home-away-from-home) having
just had himself an illicit smoke with the pigeons
out there on the 4th floor ledge and… *he's* talkin'
to me… Oh yeah… he's talkin' to *me…*

WING AND A PRAYER

Strange being middle-aged, balding,
and not just a little insignificant
and still looking up to my John
Wayne, Ted Williams dad

knowing intellectually that there
are no heroes... not really, but
having to plead guilty to the charge
of hero-worship anyway, of romancing

with my inner schoolboy heart
the mystique of your silver, B-29,
Terry and the Pirates, fly-boy story
where you, flight-suited and

bomber-jacketed in zippers and
insignia, roar the wild blue yonder
in that seat-of-the-pants, roger
wilco world of cabin pressure,

flight instruments, radar bogies,
Mae Wests, bomb-bay doors,
clamoring hearts, white knuckles,
bated breath, curses... and prayers...

WOLFEN

Graying and long-in-the-tooth, guitar case
Slung up behind him like a timber wolf's tail,
he's drawn from out of the woodwork of his
cabin-fever, backwoods-hills den along with

the legions of other lone-wolf steppenwolves
stepping up to the open-mic, each powerless in the
thrall of his particular Alpha Wolf's anthems, the
ones curled up in the lair of his skull, living there,

calls of the wild thrumming his tuning-fork
heart until he's gotta *howl*— can't *help* it any
more than the beagle scratched behind the ear
can help thumping his hind paw on the rug!

Born to be Wi-hi-ld!
Wild Thing (I think I love you!)
I see a ba-had moo-hoon risin'!
A-HOO-hoo! Werewolves in London!

He'd howl
all night long...
but for that *merciful*
three-song limit...

ZELIG

I'd see you *first!*
You'd trip my tripwire,
blip the screen of my
Distant Early Warning
radar— the 'Cold War'
never slept…

Life was the
never-ending audition,
and I wanted the part…
that *role*…
wanted *in* on your movie
needed *in* on your life

By the time you saw *me*
I'd researched you…
belly-glided over the
moon-white sand
up to the rim of
your campfire light

And soaked up your lingo
your rhythms, your inflections
your *joie de vivre*
your red flags
your *whatever* outlook,
your… *je ne sais quois*

I could do you
better than you—
we'd trade smiles…
we'd shake hands…
a friendly "Hi…"
and I was *in!*

www.ingramcontent.com/pod-product-compliance
Lightning Source LLC
LaVergne TN
LVHW021542080426
835509LV00019B/2790